Lucky

Leprechaun

Cookie

Recipes

for

St. Patrick's Day

Introduction

St. Patrick's Day is a festive time of year when everyone gets to be Irish. With good food, good drink and lots and lots of green! This recipe book contains tons of delicious traditional Irish and Leprechaun inspired cookies for you to make, bake and enjoy!

St. Patrick's Day Mint Chocolate Chip Cookies

Ingredients:

3/4 cup butter, at room temperature
2 3/4 cups flour
1 1/4 cups sugar
2 eggs
1 tsp. baking powder
1/2 tsp. salt
1 tsp. vanilla extract
green food coloring, 8 - 10 drops
2 cups andes creme de menthe baking chips

Directions:

1. Preheat oven to 375 degrees.
2. Add butter and sugar to stand mixer (I'll be using a hand mixer).
3. Cream until light and fluffy.
4. Add eggs, scrape down the sides of the bowl and mix again.
5. Add vanilla and mix until light and fluffy again.
6. Sift together flour, baking powder and salt.
7. Add to mixer and mix on low until combined.
8. Add enough green food coloring to get the right color.
9. Different brands will take different amounts, but 8 – 10 drops is about what it will take. (The color of the dough should be a little darker than you want the cookie color to be.)
10. Add mint chips and mix until incorporated.
11. Drop cookie dough by the tbsp. onto parchment paper on a baking sheet.
12. Bake for 12 – 14 minutes at 375 degrees.
13. Let cool.

Green chocolate chip cookies for St. Patrick Day

Ingredients:

1 1/2 cups all-purpose flour
1/2 tsp. baking soda
1/4 tsp. baking powder
1/2 cup butter, softened
3/4 cups white sugar
1/2 of one jumbo egg
1/2 tsp. vanilla extract
3 drops of green gel food coloring
1/2 cup semi sweet chocolate chips
1/4 cup green chocolate chips

Directions:

1. Preheat oven to 375 degrees F (190 degrees C).
2. I used non-stick cookie sheet , if you are using baking sheet line with parchment paper.
3. In a small bowl, stir together flour, baking soda, and baking powder. Set aside.
4. In a large bowl, cream together the butter and sugar until smooth.
5. Make sure not to incorporate too air by beating to long. Beat in egg, food coloring and vanilla. Gradually blend in the dry ingredients. Stir in chocolate chips.
6. Roll dough into balls about one inch in diameter and flatten slightly to create round discs, and place onto ungreased cookie sheets
7. Bake about 10 minutes in the preheated oven, or until golden around the edges.

Leprechaun Minty Swirl Cookies

Ingredients:

1 cup butter, room temperature
1 1/2 cups sugar
1 1/2 tsp. baking powder
1/2 tsp. salt
1 egg
1 tsp. mint extract
3 1/2 cups all purpose flour
3 tbsps. unsweetened cocoa powder
5-8 green gel food coloring drops
1/2 cup chocolate chips

Directions:

1. In the bowl of an electric mixer fitted with the wire attachment beat butter on medium speed until fluffy, about 30-40 seconds.
2. Scrape the bowl, and whisk in sugar, salt, baking powder and mint extract. Scrape the bowl as needed and beat until combined. Beat in the egg and when combined, replace the wire attachment with the paddle attachment and gently beat in flour. If the dough is too soft, add ½ cup of flour. The dough must have the texture of play dough.
3. Divide the dough in half, and using a spatula, knead in the green food coloring in one half.
4. Add the remaining half to the bowl of a mixer and gently beat in cocoa powder until fully combined.
5. Roll dough into two balls, cover in plastic wrap and chill in the refrigerator for 10-15 minutes so its easier to work with.
6. Cover your working area with one layer of plastic wrap, 15 - 16 inches long. Remove the dough from the refrigerator and unwrap.
7. Place the green dough ball onto the plastic wrap on the counter, flatten it and using a rolling pin shape it into a rectangular, about 10X9. Repeat with the chocolate dough ball, but make the rectangular one inch smaller.
8. Transfer the chocolate rectangle onto the green rectangle. Its ok if the dough tears down in some spots, use your fingers to shape it. The dough must be soft and easy to work with. Press the chocolate chips into the chocolate layer.

9. The chocolate rectangle is on top of the green rectangle that sits on plastic wrap. Using the plastic wrap lift the edge that is closer to you and start rolling the dough into a cookie roll. The dough now resembles a cookie roll covered in plastic wrap. You can shape it as a log, or make it more round, as you prefer. Secure the ends and place in the fridge for at least 6 hours.
10. The dough can be made in advance and left in the fridge overnight, or even for 2 days. When you are ready to bake the cookies, preheat oven to 350F. Remove the cookie roll from the refrigerator and slice in ½ or ¼ inch rounds.
11. Line two cookie sheets with parchment paper and arrange the cookies 1½ inches from each other.
12. Bake for 10 minutes. Mid baking switch the sheet trays in the oven: the upper one goes to the bottom, and the bottom one is moved up.
13. The cookies are done when the edges are firm and the bottoms light brown.
14. Remove from the oven and let the cookies cool on the cookie sheets for 2 minutes, after that transfer to a cooling rack.

St. Patrick's Day Funfetti Chocolate Chip Cookies

Ingredients:

1 ¼ cups all purpose flour
½ tsp. baking soda
½ tsp. salt
1 stick unsalted butter, at room temperature
½ cup brown sugar
½ cup granulated sugar
1 large egg
½ tsp. vanilla
½ cup chocolate chips
½ cup sprinkles, plus extra for topping

Directions:

1. In a medium bowl, sift together the flour, baking soda, and salt.
2. In a large bowl, cream together butter and sugars until light and fluffy. Add in the egg and mix until fully incorporated. Stir in the vanilla.
3. Add the dry ingredients to the wet ingredients and mix until combined. Stir in the sprinkles and chocolate chips.
4. Cover the dough, and chill for 24 - 48 hours.
5. Preheat oven to 350 degrees F.
6. Form the dough into large balls, about 2.5 tbsps. each, and space a few inches apart on a cookie sheet. If desired, roll the top of the dough balls in extra sprinkles.
7. Bake for 10 - 12 minutes, until the cookies are slightly golden brown on the edges but are still soft in the centers. Let cool on the cookie sheet for 3 minutes, then transfer to a wire rack to cool completely.

Lucky Green White Chocolate Chip Cookies

Ingredients:

1 1/3 cup all purpose flour
1/2 tsp. baking powder
1/2 tsp. baking soda
1/2 tsp. salt
1/2 cup (1 stick) butter at room temperature
1/2 cup granulated sugar
1/2 cup firmly packed light brown sugar
1 large egg
1 tsp. Vanilla extract
1/2 cup white chocolate chips
Green food coloring (about 12 drops)

Directions:

1. Preheat oven to 350 degrees. Line a baking sheet with parchment paper to make clean up easy.
2. Mix the butter and the sugars together until they are smooth. Add in the egg and vanilla and mix it until they are combined.
3. Then add in the dry ingredients - I just dump the flour, baking powder, baking soda and salt on top of the butter and sugar mixture. Gently stir the dry ingredients together first and then mix everything together.
4. At this point add in the green food coloring. I started with 6 drops and mixed them in. Then I added more drops until it reached a deep green color that I liked, which ended up being 12 drops.
5. Remember that the dough will look darker in color than it will after it is baked. So you might want to make it a little darker than you think you will need.
6. Final step - add in the white chocolate chips. Add as many as you like, I used about a 1/2 cup.
7. Shape the dough into tbsp. sized balls and place them on the parchment covered baking sheet.
8. Bake at 350 degrees for 12 to 14 minutes.

St Patrick's Day White Chocolate Chip Macadamia Cookies

Ingredients:

2 sticks + 2 tbsps. unsalted butter, soft
3/4 cup Imperial Sugar Extra Fine Granulated Sugar
3/4 cup well packed Imperial Sugar Light Brown Sugar
2 large eggs, room temperature
2 tsps. vanilla extract
3/4 tsp. salt
Few drops green food color
2 3/4 cups all-purpose flour*
1 tsp. baking soda
1 bag (12 oz.) white chocolate chunks or chips
1 cup non salted macadamia nuts
Preheat oven to 350 directions F.

Directions:

1. Cream butter until smooth, add sugars and cream further. Add eggs one at a time add vanilla and salt and mix until light and creamy. Add a few drops of green food color.
2. Sift together flour and baking soda. Add flour in one step to creamed mixture and mix until just combined. Do not over mix.
3. Add chocolate chips and macadamia nuts. Scoop dough using a large ice cream scoop.
4. Place on a parchment or silicone baking mat lined or buttered cookie sheets.
5. Bake until light golden brown, about 11-13 minutes. For soft and chewy cookies bake them until center is still soft. For a firmer cookie bake slightly longer.

St. Patrick's Shamrock Cookies

Ingredients:

1/4 cup packed brown sugar
1/4 tsp. vanilla extract
1 cup flour
1/4 tsp. salt
1/2 cup butter or margarine, softened

Directions:

1. Preheat oven to 325°F
2. In a medium bowl, beat butter or margarine and brown sugar with an electric mixer on medium speed until light and fluffy.
3. Stir in vanilla.
4. Add flour and salt to the butter and blend well.
5. With a rolling pin on a lightly floured surface, roll out dough 1/4-inch thick.
6. Cut out cookies using a 3 inch Shamrock cookie cutter and place 2 inches apart on ungreased cookie sheets.
7. Re-roll scraps.
8. Sprinkle green sugar crystals on each cookie.
9. Bake 20 to 25 minutes, until cookies are pale golden, not brown.
10. Let stand 2 minutes.
11. Remove to a rack and let cool completely.

Irish Shamrock Cookies

Ingredients:

1/2 cup butter, softened
1 (3 oz.) package instant pistachio pudding mix
1 1/3 cups baking mix
1 egg
1 tbsp. white sugar

Directions:

1. Preheat oven to 350 degrees F (175 degrees C). Lightly grease baking sheet.
2. Cream together the butter or margarine and the pudding mix.
3. Blend in the baking mix, egg and sugar and mix well.
4. On a lightly floured surface roll out the dough to 3/8 inch thickness and cut into cookies with a shamrock cookie cutter.
5. Place cookies on the prepared baking sheet and bake at 350 degrees F (175 degrees C) for 9 to 10 minutes or until lightly browned on the edges. Let cookies cool on rack. Frost with green colored icing if desired.

Irish Potatoes

Ingredients:

1 cup confectioners' sugar
1 cup shredded coconut
1 1/2 tbsps. cream
2 tbsps. ground cinnamon

Directions:

1. Sprinkle the sugar on the coconut.
2. Add the cream and mix gently.
3. Take approximately 1/2 tbsp. of dough and roll into balls.
4. Place cinnamon in a plastic bag and shake cookies a few at a time until coated.

Irish Ginger Snaps

Ingredients:

1 cup white sugar
1 egg
1/4 tsp. salt
3/4 cup shortening
2 cups all-purpose flour
1/2 tsp. baking soda
1 tsp. ground cloves
1 tsp. ground ginger
1 tsp. ground cinnamon

Directions:

1. Preheat oven to 350 degrees F (175 degrees C).
2. Cream sugar, egg, salt and shortening together.
3. Add flour, baking soda and spices. Mix well.
4. Roll teaspoonfuls of dough into balls and roll the balls in sugar.
5. Bake at 350 degrees F (175 degrees C) for 5 to 6 minutes.

Irish Soda Bread Cookies

Ingredients:

2 cups all-purpose flour
3/4 cup white sugar
1/2 tsp. baking soda
1/2 cup butter
1/2 cup dried currants
1/4 cup buttermilk
1 egg
1/4 tsp. salt
1 tsp. caraway seed

Directions:

1. Preheat oven to 350 degrees F (175 degrees C).
2. Combine dry ingredients in a mixing bowl. With a pastry blender, cut in butter until mixture resembles coarse meal. Stir in currants.
3. Mix in beaten egg. Pour in milk and mix with a fork to make a soft dough (may need a little more milk).
4. On a floured surface, shape dough into a ball and knead lightly 5 or 6 times. Roll out dough to 1/4 inch thick and cut into squares and triangles with a knife (approximately 2 inches in diameter).
5. Bake for 12 to 14 minutes or until slightly browned.

Irish Flag Cookies

Ingredients:

1 cup butter
1 1/2 cups confectioners' sugar
1 egg
1 tsp. vanilla extract
2 1/2 cups all-purpose flour
1 tsp. baking soda
1 tsp. cream of tartar

Directions:

1. In a large bowl, cream together butter and confectioners' sugar. Beat in egg and vanilla extract. Mix well.
2. In a medium sized bowl, stir together the flour, baking soda and cream of tartar.
3. Blend into the butter mixture. Divide dough into thirds and shape into balls.
4. Working with 1/3 of the dough at a time, roll out dough to 1/4 inch thick on a floured surface. With a knife, cut dough into rectangles about 2 inches high by 3 inches long. (6 x 8 cm).
5. Place rectangles on an ungreased cookie sheet, 2 inches apart. Bake in a preheated 350 degree F (175 degrees C) oven until lightly browned. Cool completely on wire rack.

Irish Whiskey Caramel Thumbprint Cookies

Cookie Ingredients:

1 cup unsalted butter, softened
1/3 cup granulated sugar
1/3 cup light brown sugar, packed
1 tsp. Vanilla
1 tsp. Jameson irish whiskey
2 cups all-purpose flour
1/2 cup semi-sweet mini chocolate chips, frozen

Filling Ingredients:

1 (11-oz.) Bag vanilla caramels, unwrapped
3 tbsps. heavy whipping cream
2 tbsps. Jameson Irish whiskey
Ground sea salt

Directions:

1. Preheat oven to 350 degrees.
2. Cream the butter and sugars together, on medium speed, for 2 minutes.
3. Add the vanilla and whiskey; mix for 1 minute.
4. Slowly add the flour, on low-speed; mix just until the majority of the flour is incorporated.
5. Using a spatula, mix in the mini chocolate chips.
6. Roll dough into 24 equal sized balls, around 1 1/2-inches wide, and then place on a Silpat or parchment paper lined baking sheet. Using your thumb, make an indentation in the middle of each cookie.
7. Bake for 10 minutes, or just until the bottom edges of the cookies start turning a golden brown.
8. After removing the cookies from the oven, use the back of a spoon to reinforce the indentation in each cookie. Allow cookies to cool on the baking sheet for 3 minutes, before removing to a cooling rack.
9. Melt the caramels into the cream, over medium-low heat, stirring constantly. This will take several minutes, so be patient; your arm will definitely get a workout.
10. Take the caramel off of the heat and add the whiskey. Be very careful; the caramel will bubble up with the addition of the whiskey; hot caramel is like liquid lava when it hits your skin.

11. With a spoon, or a decorating bottle, fill the indentation of each cookie with caramel, and then top with a bit of the ground sea salt.
12. Allow the cookies to rest for several hours before placing in an airtight container, with waxed paper between each layer of cookies.

Irish Coconut Cookies

Ingredients:

½ cup butter, softened
½ cup caster sugar
1 medium egg
½ cup plain flour
½ cup dessicated coconut

Directions:

1. Preheat your oven to 350 degrees F. (180 degrees C.) and line a baking tray with non stick grease proof paper.
2. Lash all the ingredients into a large bowl and beat well until you have a dough.
3. Using a tbsp. as a size measure, spoon out the cookie dough and space well on the baking tray.
4. Bake the cookies in the oven for 15 minutes or until golden brown.
5. Allow to cool on the tray before serving.

Irish Creme Mocha Thumbprint Cookies

Ingredients:

2 cups all-purpose flour
1/2 cup unsweetened dutch-process cocoa powder
2 tbsps. espresso powder
1/2 tsp. salt
1 cup + 1 tbsp. butter, at room temperature
1 cup sugar
1 large egg, at room temperature
1 tsp. vanilla extract

Filling Ingredients:

4 oz. white chocolate chips
1 tbsp. butter, softened
1/4 cup heavy cream
2 tbsps. Irish Creme coffee creamer
1/2 cup sifted confectioners' sugar

Directions:

1. Whisk the flour, cocoa, espresso and salt together in a medium bowl.
2. In a separate large bowl beat the butter and granulated sugar together on medium speed about 3 minutes until pale and fluffy. Scrape down the sides of the bowl.
3. Beat in the egg and vanilla.
4. On low speed beat in the flour mixture until just combined.
5. Roll the dough into 1-inch balls and place on a large parchment lined baking sheet or two. Use your finger or the end of a wooden spoon or ice cream scoop to press a well into the center of each one.
6. Refrigerate the cookies 30 minutes.
7. Preheat the oven to 350 degrees F. Line a baking sheet or two with silpats or parchment and set cookies on it an inch apart (return the remaining unbaked cookies back to the fridge).
8. Bake 7 minutes. Press the end of a wooden spoon or cookie scoop into the well in the center again. Cool completely on the baking sheet. Repeat until all the cookies are baked.

Filling Directions:

1. Place the white chocolate chips and butter in a small heat-proof bowl.
2. Heat the heavy cream and creamer together in a small saucepan over medium – high heat, stirring often, until it comes to a boil.
3. Pour over the chocolate chips and cover the bowl tightly with aluminum foil. Let it sit five minutes.
4. Whisk until the chocolate is completely melted and smooth.
5. Add the sugar and whisk well until smooth and creamy.
6. Spoon into the wells of the cookies.
7. Let set 1 hour.

Shamrock Stained Glass Window Cookies

Ingredients:

1 cup sugar
3/4 cup butter or margarine, softened
1 tsp. vanilla
2 eggs
2 1/2 cups all-purpose flour
1 tsp. baking powder
1/4 tsp. salt
4 rolls (1 oz. each) fruit flavored hard candies (green colored for Irish)
Shamrock shaped cookie cutter

Directions:

1. In large bowl, beat sugar, butter, vanilla and eggs with electric mixer on medium speed, or mix with spoon. Stir in flour, baking powder and salt. Cover; refrigerate about 1 hour or until firm.
2. Heat oven to 375 degrees F.
3. Cover cookie sheet with parchment paper or foil.
4. On lightly floured cloth-covered surface, roll one-third of dough at a time 1/8 inch thick.
5. Cut into desired shapes with shamrock shaped cookie cutter.
6. Cut shapes from centers of cookies such as a square or small circle.
7. Place cookies on parchment paper.
8. Place whole or partially crushed pieces of candy in cutouts, depending on size and shape of design.
9. Leave pieces as large as possible because candy melts easily. Do not use fine candy "dust.
10. To crush candy, place in heavy plastic bag and tap lightly with rolling pin.) Place cutouts from centers of cookies on top of candies, if desired.
11. Bake 7 to 9 minutes or until cookies are very light brown and candy is melted.
12. If candy has not completely spread within cutout design, immediately spread with knife.
13. Cool completely on parchment paper, about 30 minutes. Gently remove cookies to cooling rack.

Blarney Stones

Ingredients:

2 cups confectioners' sugar
1/2 cup milk, or as needed
1 1/2 tsps. vanilla extract
2 cups dry roasted salted peanuts, finely chopped
1 pound cake, cut into bite-sized cubes

Directions:

1. Pour confectioners' sugar in a bowl. Gradually add milk, whisking constantly, until mixture has a thin frosting consistency; whisk in vanilla extract.
2. Place chopped peanuts in a bowl. Line a flat surface or a plate with waxed paper.
3. Dip 1 pound cake cube in frosting and roll cube in peanuts; place on wax paper to dry. Repeat with remaining pound cake pieces.

Cream Cheese Sugar Cookies

Ingredients:

1 cup white sugar
1 cup butter, softened
1 (3 oz.) package cream cheese, softened
1/2 tsp. salt
1/2 tsp. almond extract
1/2 tsp. vanilla extract
1 egg yolk
2 1/4 cups all-purpose flour

Directions:

1. In a large bowl, combine the sugar, butter, cream cheese, salt, almond and vanilla extracts, and egg yolk. Beat until smooth.
2. Stir in flour until well blended. Chill the dough for 8 hours, or overnight.
3. Preheat oven to 375 degrees F (190 degrees C).
4. On a lightly floured surface, roll out the dough 1/3 at a time to 1/8 inch thickness, refrigerating remaining dough until ready to use.
5. Cut into shamrocks with lightly floured cookie cutters.
6. Place 1 inch apart on ungreased cookie sheets.
7. Leave cookies plain for frosting, or brush with slightly beaten egg white and sprinkle with green sprinkles or green colored sugar.
8. Bake for 7 to 10 minutes in the preheated oven, or until light and golden brown.
9. Cool cookies completely before frosting.

Pot of Gold Rainbow Cookies

Ingredients:

8 oz. almond paste
1 cup butter, softened
1 cup white sugar
4 eggs, separated
2 cups all-purpose flour
6 drops red food coloring
6 drops green food coloring
1/4 cup seedless red raspberry jam
1/4 cup apricot jam
1 cup semisweet chocolate chips, melted

Directions:

1. Preheat oven to 350 degrees F (175 degrees C). Line three 9x13 inch baking pans with parchment paper.
2. In a large bowl, break apart almond paste with a fork, and cream together with butter, sugar, and egg yolks. When mixture is fluffy and smooth, stir in flour to form a dough. In a small bowl, beat egg whites until soft peaks form. Fold egg whites into the dough. Divide dough into 3 equal portions. Mix one portion with red food coloring, and one with green food coloring. Spread each portion into one of the prepared baking pans.
3. Bake 10 to 12 minutes in the preheated oven, until lightly browned. Carefully remove from pan and parchment paper, and cool completely on wire racks.
4. Place green layer onto a piece of plastic wrap large enough to wrap all three layers. Spread green layer with raspberry jam, and top with uncolored layer.
5. Spread with apricot jam, and top with pink layer. Transfer layers to a baking sheet, and enclose with plastic wrap.
6. Place a heavy pan or cutting board on top of wrapped layers to compress. Chill in the refrigerator 8 hours, or overnight.
7. Remove plastic wrap.
8. Top with melted chocolate chips, and refrigerate 1 hour, or until chocolate is firm.
9. Slice into small squares to serve.

St. Patrick's Day Zucchini-Oatmeal Cookies

Ingredients:

1/2 cup butter
3/4 cup white sugar
1 egg
1/2 tsp. vanilla extract
1 1/2 cups grated zucchini
1 1/2 cups all-purpose flour
1/2 tsp. baking soda
1 tsp. ground cinnamon
1 cup quick cooking oats
1 cup granola
2 cups semisweet chocolate chips

Directions:

1. Preheat oven to 350 degrees F (175 degrees C).
2. In a medium bowl, cream butter and sugar until fluffy.
3. Stir in the egg and vanilla, mix well, then stir in the shredded zucchini. Sift together the flour, baking soda and cinnamon, stir into the zucchini mixture.
4. Finally, stir in the oats, granola and chocolate chips.
5. Drop dough from a tsp. onto an unprepared cookie sheet.
6. Leave at least 2 inches between cookies.
7. Bake for 10 to 12 minutes in the preheated oven. The cookies will stay soft and moist because of the zucchini.

Irish Coffee Meringues

Meringues Ingredients:

7 tbsps. sugar
3 tbsps. (packed) dark brown sugar
1 tsp. instant espresso powder or instant coffee powder
2 large egg whites

Filling Ingredients:

1 1/4 cups chilled whipping cream
2 tbsps. sugar
2 tbsps. Irish whiskey
2 tsps. instant espresso powder or instant coffee powder
Chocolate-covered coffee beans (optional)

Meringues Directions:

1. Preheat oven to 250°F. Line 2 heavy baking sheets with parchment paper. Stir 3 tbsps. sugar, 1 tbsp. brown sugar and 1 tsp. instant espresso powder in small bowl to blend well. Using hand-held electric mixer, beat egg whites in medium bowl until medium-stiff peaks form. Add remaining 4 tbsps. sugar and 2 tbsps. dark brown sugar to egg whites by tablespoonfuls and beat until stiff peaks form. Fold coffee-sugar mixture into meringue.
2. Drop meringue by rounded tablespoonfuls onto prepared baking sheets, spacing evenly. Using knife, gently spread meringues 2 1/2- to 3-inch rounds. Bake until meringues are dry and can be easily be lifted from parchment, about 45 minutes. Transfer meringues to racks and cool completely. (Can be prepared 2 days ahead. Store in airtight containers at room temperature.)

Filling Directions:

1. Beat 1 cup whipping cream in medium bowl to medium-firm peaks. Add sugar, Irish whiskey and instant espresso powder and beat until firm peaks form.
2. Place 1 meringue on plate, flat side down. Spoon 1 generous tbsp. of espresso cream filling over. Top with another meringue, flat side down, and press gently until filling spreads to edge. Repeat with remaining meringues and filling. (Can be prepared 1 hour ahead. Cover with plastic wrap and refrigerate.)

3. Beat remaining 1/4 cup whipping cream in small bowl until firm peaks form. Spoon small dollop of cream atop each meringue. Garnish each with chocolate-covered coffee beans, if desired.

Leprechaun Minty Chocolatey Chippy Meringue Cookies

Ingredients:

2 large egg whites – room temperature
1/8 tsp. salt
½ cup Superfine or Caster Sugar – If you don't have it, watch my video on how to make it at home
½ tsp. peppermint extract
1/8 tsp. green food coloring or color of your choice (Pink) (optional)
½ cup mini semi-sweet chocolate chips

Directions:

1. Preheat oven to 225 degrees F. Place cooking rack in center of oven.
2. Line a baking sheet with parchment paper
3. Place egg whites into a clean bowl. Note: A plastic bowl is not recommended, as plastic retains residues, which can prevent the eggs from developing into firm peaks.
4. Using a stand mixer or hand mixer, beat the egg whites on medium speed, until they get foamy. You can do this by hand, but it will just take a bit longer, so be ready for an arm workout.
5. Once foamy, add the salt. Continue to beat until soft peaks form. See video.
6. With the mixer on medium-low, gradually add the sugar about 1 tbsp. at a time. Once half of the sugar has been added, scrape down the bowl. Continue to add the rest of the sugar. Once all sugar has been added, scrape again. Wash you spatula, to remove the sugar. You don't want that to get back into the meringue. Beat until firm peaks form and meringue is smooth when you run it between your fingers.
7. Add the peppermint extract, with the mixer on low and beat to combine. Don't worry if the peppermint smell seems overpowering, as it fades with cooking, so it's not too much.
8. With the mixer off, add the green food coloring if desired. Mix to combine. You may need to finish it by hand, as some may get on the sides of the bowl or not get to the bottom.
9. Pour chocolate chips into the bowl and fold in with a spatula.
10. If desired, spoon mixture into a piping bag with a wide tip or a plastic bag with the corner cut off. Gently shake down the meringue to the bottom of the bag and twist the bag. See video. If not using a bag, grab two spoons.

11. Onto the baking sheet, pipe or spoon the meringue about 2 inches apart. Secure the parchment to the baking sheet with a few dabs of the meringue on each corner.
12. Place baking sheet on the center rack of preheated oven.
13. After 45 minutes turn the oven off, but DO NOT open the door!
14. Leave the meringues in the oven undisturbed for at least 3-4 hours, but preferably overnight.
15. Once the meringues have dried, remove from baking sheet.

Pistachio and Chocolate Leprechaun Cookies

Ingredients:

1 cup butter, softened
1/2 cup granulated sugar
1/2 cup light brown sugar
1 tsp. vanilla extract
1/2 tsp. almond extract
1 (3.4 oz.) package instant pistachio pudding (dry mix)
2 eggs
2 1/4 cups all-purpose flour
1 tsp. baking soda
1/4 tsp. salt
1/2 cup dark chocolate chips
1/2 cup green M&Ms
1/2 cup chopped walnuts
Green food coloring

Directions:

1. Preheat oven to 375 degrees F. In an electric mixer with paddle attachment, cream together butter and sugars. Add extracts and pudding mix and eggs one at a time. Beat for 1 minute.
2. In a separate bowl, combine flour, baking soda, and salt. Add to sugar mixture one a little at a time, mixing thoroughly between each addition. Add a drop or two of green food coloring at this point if you want a stronger green color. Stir in chocolate chips, green M&Ms, chopped walnuts, and any other mix-ins you like!
3. Bake for 8-10 minutes or until edges are turning slightly golden.
4. Let cool and enjoy!

Nutty Buddy Leprechaun Cookies

Ingredients:

Nutter Butter cookies
Orange chocolate melts
Green chocolate melts
chocolate chips, and
Spring sprinkles with green flower shapes, white circles and pink hearts

Directions:

1. Melt the melts in a bowl or mug in the microwave in 10 second bursts.
2. Dip one end of the Nutter Butter in orange melts for the beard.
3. Use a spoon to smear some up the sides as sideburns for the leprechaun.
4. Dip the other end in the green melts for the hat.
5. Lay your leprechauns on a piece of wax paper to allow the chocolate to harden.
6. When the chhocolate has hardened on the cookies, melt some more green and put some of the green chocolate in a plastic bag.
7. Snip off the corner to pipe on a stripe of green for the brim of the hat.
8. Melt some chocolate chips.
9. Put the melted chocolate chips in another bag and snip off the corner.
10. Make a thin brown stripe right above the green brim for the strap of the hat.
11. I repeated the step with melted chocolate chips in another bag to make a stripe of brown right above the stripe of green. This was the strap on his hat.
12. Use melted chocolate to attach the sprinkles.
13. A green flower sprinkle goes in the center for the strap of the hat as a clover.
14. Two white circle sprinkles are used for eyes.
15. An upside down heart is attached for the mouth.
16. Dip a tootpick in melted chocolate chips and create dots for pupils on the eyes.

Lucky Leprechaun Cookies Recipe

Ingredients:

1-1/2 cups butter, softened
1-1/2 cups sugar
2 eggs
3 tsps. vanilla extract
4 cups all-purpose flour
1 tsp. baking soda
1 tsp. cream of tartar
1 tsp. salt
3 to 4 cups Royal Icing
Assorted paste food coloring
Green shimmer dust or edible glitter
Green shamrock sprinkles, optional
Miniature semisweet chocolate chips

Directions:

1. In a large bowl, cream butter and sugar until light and fluffy. Add eggs, one at a time, beating well after each addition. Beat in vanilla. Combine the flour, baking soda, cream of tartar and salt; gradually add to the creamed mixture. Cover and refrigerate for 30 minutes or until easy to handle.
2. Preheat oven to 350°. On a lightly floured surface, roll out dough to 1/4-in. thickness. For leprechauns, cut out dough with lightly floured 5-in. gingerbread boy cookie cutter. If desired, trim leprechaun's body for a thinner shape.
3. For each hat, cut a 1-1/2-in. square and a 1-3/4x1/4-in. brim from dough scraps. Place leprechauns 2 in. apart on ungreased baking sheets. Place hat squares and brims above heads, shaping gently to touch the heads.
4. Bake 10-14 minutes or until edges are lightly browned. Cool 1 minute before carefully removing to wire racks to cool completely.
5. Tint small amounts of Royal Icing red, yellow and black.
6. Leave a small amount plain. Tint remaining icing green and orange. Frost leprechauns; decorate with shimmer dust and shamrock sprinkles if desired. For eyes, attach miniature chocolate chips with plain frosting.

Leprechaun Hat Cookies

Ingredients:

1 pouch sugar cookie mix
1/2 cup butter or margarine, softened
1 egg
1 container creamy vanilla frosting
1/4 tsp. green gel food color
24 large marshmallows
24 small (1-inch) chewy chocolate candies
12 small green gumdrops

Directions:

1. Heat oven to 375 degrees F. In medium bowl, stir cookie mix, butter and egg until soft dough forms. Roll dough in 24 (1-inch) balls. On ungreased cookie sheets, place 2 inches apart.
2. 2 Bake 10 to 12 minutes or until edges are light golden brown. Immediately place marshmallow on each cookie. Remove from cookie sheets to cooling racks. Cool completely, about 15 minutes.
3. 3 In microwavable bowl, microwave frosting on High 30 seconds. Stir; frosting should be a thick spoonable glaze. Stir food color into frosting, adding more if needed to achieve desired color. Spoon warm frosting over each cookie, coating completely and allowing excess to drip off. Let stand 20 minutes to set.
4. 4 Roll chocolate candies into ropes. Flatten with rolling pin into 1/8-inch-thick ribbons. Cut into strips with scissors to resemble hat bands; arrange around base of marshmallow on each cookie. Cut gumdrops crosswise in half (reshaping as needed). Press cut side onto hat band. Lift cookies onto serving platter with pancake turner, leaving excess frosting behind. Store in airtight container.

Irish Minty Pinwheels

Ingredients:

1 pouch (1 lb. 1.5 oz.) sugar cookie mix
1/2 cup butter or margarine, softened
1 egg
1/4 cup unsweetened baking cocoa
2 tbsps. Gold Medal™ all-purpose flour
1/2 tsp. mint extract
2 to 3 drops green food color

Directions:

1. In large bowl, stir cookie mix, butter and egg until dough forms.
2. Divide dough in half. Stir cocoa into one half. Stir flour, mint extract and food color into other half. Place chocolate dough on 17x12-inch sheet waxed paper. Top dough with second sheet of waxed paper. Roll dough to form 12x7-inch rectangle. Repeat with green colored dough.
3. Remove top sheet of waxed paper from both doughs. Using waxed paper to lift green dough, invert onto chocolate dough. Gently press layered dough to 14x8-inch rectangle. Remove top sheet waxed paper. Use bottom sheet waxed paper to help roll doughs up together tightly, beginning at long side. Wrap tightly in waxed paper; freeze at least 2 hours or until very firm.
4. Heat oven to 375°F. Unwrap dough; cut into 1/4-inch slices. Place slices about 2 inches apart on ungreased cookie sheet. Bake 9 to 11 minutes or until set. Cool 2 minutes; remove from cookie sheet to wire rack.

Irish Chocolate-Mint Thumbprints

Ingredients:

1 cup butter, softened
1 cup powdered sugar
1 1/2 tsps. peppermint extract
2 egg yolks
16 drops green food color
2 1/4 cups all-purpose flour
1/2 tsp. baking powder
1/4 tsp. salt
3/4 cup dark chocolate chips
3 tbsps. whipping cream
3 tbsps. butter
18 thin rectangular crème de menthe chocolate candies, unwrapped, cut in half diagonally

Directions:

1. Heat oven to 350°F. Line cookie sheets with cooking parchment paper.
2. In large bowl, beat 1 cup butter and the powdered sugar with electric mixer on medium speed until light and fluffy. Beat in peppermint extract, egg yolks and food color until blended. On low speed, beat in flour, baking powder and salt.
3. Shape dough into 1-inch balls; place 2 inches apart on cookie sheets.
4. Using end of handle of wooden spoon, press a deep well into center of each cookie.
5. Bake 10 to 12 minutes or until set. Reshape wells with end of handle of wooden spoon. Cool 2 minutes; remove from cookie sheets to cooling racks. Cool completely, about 15 minutes.
6. In medium microwavable bowl, microwave chocolate chips, cream and 3 tbsps. butter on High 1 minute, stirring frequently, until chocolate is melted and mixture is smooth. Fill each well with about 1 tsp. chocolate mixture; garnish with candy piece. Let stand about 1 hour until chocolate is set.

Irish Mint-Filled Chocolate Thumbprints

Cookie Ingredients:

1/2 cup granulated sugar
1 cup butter or margarine, softened
1 tsp. vanilla
1 egg yolk
1 1/2 cups Gold Medal™ all-purpose flour
1/4 cup unsweetened baking cocoa

Mint Filling Ingredients:

1/4 cup butter or margarine, softened
1 cup powdered sugar
1 tbsp. milk
1/4 tsp. peppermint extract
2 drops green food color
1/4 cup semisweet chocolate chips
1/4 tsp. shortening

Directions:

1. Heat oven to 375°F (if using dark or nonstick cookie sheet, heat oven to 350°F). In large bowl, beat granulated sugar, 1 cup butter and the vanilla with electric mixer on medium speed until fluffy. Beat in egg yolk until smooth. Beat in flour and cocoa.
2. Shape dough by rounded teaspoonfuls into 1-inch balls. On ungreased cookie sheet, place balls 1 inch apart. With index finger or thumb, make indentation in center of each ball.
3. Bake 7 to 9 minutes or until set. Immediately remove from cookie sheet to wire rack. Cool completely, about 30 minutes.
4. 4 In small bowl, beat 1/4 cup butter and the powdered sugar on low speed until smooth. Beat in milk, peppermint extract and enough food color for desired color. Spoon about 1/2 tsp. filling into each cookie.
5. Place chocolate chips and shortening in small resealable food-storage plastic bag; seal bag. Microwave on High about 1 minute or until softened. Gently squeeze bag until chocolate is smooth; cut off tiny corner of bag. Squeeze bag to drizzle chocolate over cookies. Let stand about 1 hour or until chocolate is set.

Lucky Leprechaun Cookie Bark

Ingredients:

14 whole Thin Mints or Mint Oreos, broken up.
1½ cup pretzels, broken into pieces.
1 lb. white chocolate, almond bark or melts
1 cup green M & M's , mint flavored or regular.
Green and white sprinkles

Directions:

1. Cover a large cookie sheet with wax paper
2. Spread broken cookies, pretzels and about ¾ C of the M & M's onto the waxed paper
3. Place white chocolate in a container and microwave for 1½ minutes
4. Stir and then microwave for another 30 seconds until melted and smooth
5. White chocolate melts faster and burns easier than chocolate
6. Drizzle the melted chocolate over the cookie mixture, spreading with spatula if needed to coat evenly
7. Sprinkle remaining M & M's and colored sprinkles over the chocolate while it is still wet
8. Do not let it harden
9. Place cookie tray into refrigerator until set and firm
10. Remove and gently break bark into small pieces
11. Store in air tight container

Lucky Leprechaun Cookies

Ingredients:

1/2 cup (1 stick) butter, room temperature
1/2 cup granulated sugar
1/4 cup vegetable oil
2 oz water
1 egg
2- 3.4 oz packages pistachio pudding mix
1/2 tsp. pure almond extract
1/2 tsp. salt
1 tsp. baking powder
2 cups all-purpose flour
Green decorating sugar

Directions:

1. Preheat the oven to 350 F degrees.
2. Beat butter, sugar, and vegetable oil in a bowl till combined.
3. Add water and egg, beating until smooth.
4. Add pudding mix, almond extract, salt and baking powder, beating until smooth; stir in flour.
5. Scoop dough by the tsp., rolling in the palm of your hands to form smooth balls; place on parchment lined baking sheet.
6. Using the bottom of a glass, dip in green decorating sugar and slightly press down on tops of cookies.
7. Bake at 350 for 11-12 minutes.
8. Remove warm cookies from baking sheet and let cool completely on cooling rack.

Hills of Ireland Cookies

Ingredients:

1 (18.25 oz.) box French vanilla cake mix
6 tbsps. butter
2 eggs
60 drops green food coloring
1 cup powdered sugar
1 tsp. corn starch

Directions:

1. Preheat the oven to 375 degrees F.
2. Melt the butter and set aside to cool.
3. In a shallow dish, mix together the powdered sugar and cornstarch with a fork.
4. In a large bowl, mix together the cooled butter, cake mix and eggs.
5. This will be a little hard to stir together.
6. Add the green food coloring and make sure it is all mixed in.
7. Take two spoons and drop a blob of dough in the powdered sugar.
8. Move it around with spoon until it is mostly covered in powdered sugar.
9. Once it is covered, roll it into a ball and place it on a cookie sheet.
10. Bake for about 9 minutes.
11. Make sure you don't over crowd the baking sheet because these cookies spread out.
12. Take them out of the oven and cool for one minute.
13. Then move onto a cooling rack.

Irish Guinness Cookies

Guinness Mixture Ingredients:

1(11.2 oz.) bottle of Guinness™ Beer
1/3 cup brown sugar

Cookie Dough Ingredients:

2cups Gold Medal™ All Purpose Flour
1 cup cocoa powder, sifted
1teaspoon baking soda
1/2 tsp. salt
1cup butter, softened
1 cup brown sugar
1/2cup granulated sugar
2 large eggs, at room temperature
1teaspoon vanilla extract
1 1/4 cups dark chocolate chips
1cup milk chocolate chips
1/2 cup mini semi-sweet chocolate chips

Directions:

1. For the Guinness™ mixture: In a saucepan over medium heat, cook the Guinness™ and brown sugar together for 20 minutes. The mixture will reduce to 1/3 cup. Set aside to cool.
2. For the Cookie Dough: In a medium bowl, mix together flour, cocoa powder, baking soda, and salt. Set aside. In the bowl of an electric mixer, beat butter for 2 minutes. Add sugars and beat for another 4 minutes. Add eggs and vanilla; mix for 2 minutes until fully incorporated. Mix in the Guinness™ mixture. Slowly add the dry ingredients into the wet ingredients, until just combined. Fold in chocolate and let chill at least 2 hours, or up to 2 days.
3. Preheat oven to 350°F. Line a baking sheet with parchment paper. Using a scoop, place rounded balls of dough on sheet, about 2 inches apart. Place more chocolate on top of each for looks, if you would like. Bake for 9 minute. Dough will be just set; let cool for 10 minutes on cookie sheet before transferring to a cooling rack.

Chocolate Guinness cookies with Bailey's Frosting

Ingredients:

1 cup unsalted butter, at room temp
1 cup white sugar
1 cup brown sugar
2 eggs
½ cup Guinness
2½ cups flour
⅔ cup cocoa
1 tsp baking soda
½ tsp salt
For the Irish buttercream frosting:
4 cups powdered sugar
2 sticks unsalted butter, at room temp
3 tbsp Bailey's Irish cream
2 tbsp milk

Directions:

1. Preheat oven to 350 degrees F.
2. Mix the cream, butter, sugar, eggs and Guinness in a mixer, on medium, until light and fluffy.
3. In a separate bowl, sift together the flour, cocoa, baking soda, salt.
4. Add the flour mixture by the tbsp. to the sugar, egg, and Guinness mixture. Mix at a medium speed until it comes together.
5. Refrigerate for one hour.
6. Drop a heaped tbsp. onto cookie sheets.
7. Back for 13 minutes.
8. Take out of the oven and let them rest.
9. Place all the frosting ingredients into a mixer and beat until light and fluffy.
10. Spread on cooled cookies.

Guinness Gingerbread Cookies

Ingredients:

1 cup Guinness Extra Stout
1/2 cup canola oil
1 3/4 cups powdered sugar
1/4 cup molasses
2 cups whole wheat flour
1/2 tsp. each baking powder, baking soda, and salt
1/2 tsp. nutmeg, cloves, and cinnamon
1 1/2 tsps. ground ginger
1 tsp. grated fresh ginger (optional)
2 tbsps. egg replacer
1 tsp. vanilla extract

Directions:

1. Simmer the cup of Guinness Extra stout uncovered on the stove top until it is reduced by half, which took me about 25 minutes. Let cool.
2. Mix together the flour, baking powder, baking soda, salt, and spices, set aside.
3. Mix together the oil and 3/4 cups of the powdered sugar, then add the molasses and 1/4 cup of the Guinness. (Save the rest of this reduction of Guinness for the icing).
4. Stir in the grated ginger if using, and gradually fold in the dry ingredients until it makes a nice coherent dough.
5. Divide the dough into two balls, wrap in plastic wrap, and refrigerate for 1 hour (up to a couple days).
6. Preheat the oven to 350°F. Spray a large piece of aluminum foil with cooking spray. Place one ball of dough on it, work it with your hand into a disk, and then roll out until very thin. It's ok if the edges crack a little, but if they are seriously ripping then let the dough warm up for about 10 minutes, then try again.
7. Cut out shapes with cookie cutters. Gently peel up the excess dough, leaving the cut out shapes on the foil. This way you don't need to handle the shapes and risk breaking them. Move aluminum foil onto a cookie sheet and bake for 5-7 minutes, until fragrant. Gather the dough scraps into a ball and repeat on a new piece of foil.
8. When the first round of cookies are done, wait a minute to cool, then transfer cookies to wire rack. You can keep using the same two pieces of foil, just re-spray with Pam each time.
9. Guinness Royal icing:

10. Whisk together egg replacer and the reduction of Guinness until quite frothy and thick.
11. Add the extract and powdered sugar.
12. Place icing in a pastry bag or plastic bag with just a snip of the corner cut off. Wait until the cookies are completely cool to decorate. The icing dries quickly, so this amount will ice one half of the cookie recipe. Make another batch of icing if you are baking both balls of dough at once. Once the icing is dry, keep the cookies in an airtight container.

About the Author

Laura Sommers is the Zombie Prepper Mom!

Helping you prepare for the Zombie Apocalypse! She is the #1 Best Selling Author of the "Recipes for the Zombie Apocalypse" cookbook series as well as over 40 other recipe books.

She is a loving wife and mother who lives on a small farm in Baltimore County, Maryland and has a passion for all things domestic especially when it comes to saving money. She has a profitable eBay business and is a couponing addict. Follow her tips and tricks to learn how to make delicious meals on a budget, save money or to learn the latest life hack!

Visit her Amazon Author Page to see her latest books:

amazon.com/author/laurasommers

Visit her blog for more life hacks or money saving ideas:

http://zombiepreppermom.blogspot.com/

Visit her on Facebook for up to date notices on what the Zombie Prepper Mom has cooking!

https://www.facebook.com/zombiepreppermom

Follow the Zombie Prepper Mom on Twitter:

http://www.twitter.com/zombieprepmom

Other books by Laura Sommers

- Easy to Make Party Dip Recipes: Chips and Dips and Salsa and Whips!
- Super Slimming Vegan Soup Recipes!
- Popcorn Lovers Recipe Book
- Inexpensive Low Carb Recipes
- Recipes for the Zombie Apocalypse: Cooking Meals with Shelf Stable Foods
- Best Traditional Irish Recipes for St. Patrick's Day
- Awesome Sugar Free Diabetic Pie Recipes

May all of your meals be a banquet
with good friends and good food.

Made in United States
Orlando, FL
05 September 2024